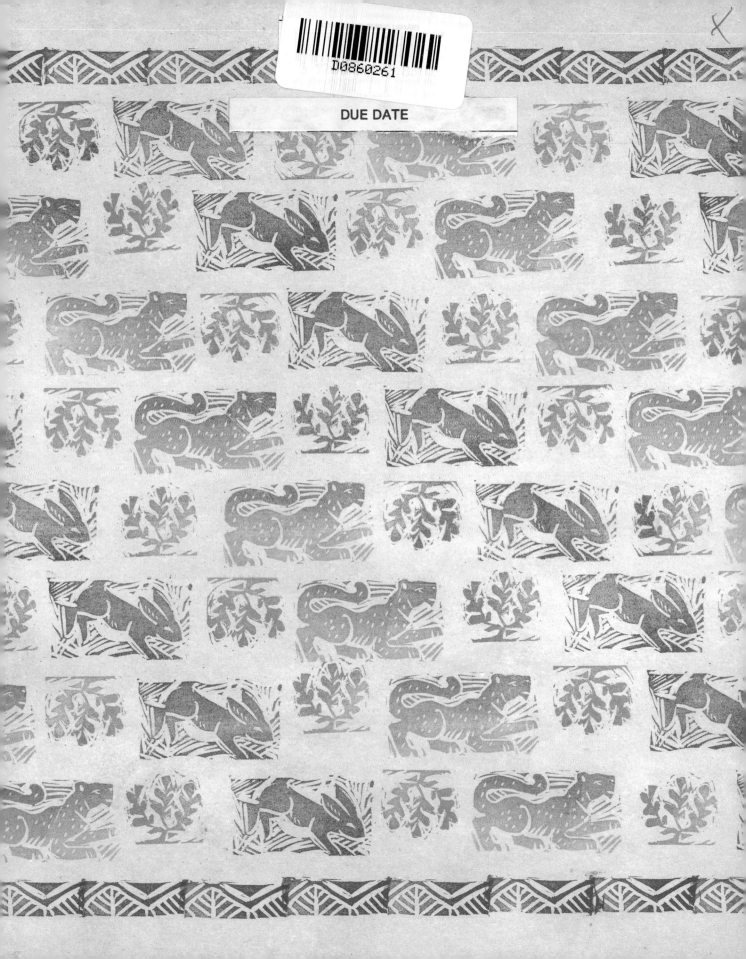

D0860261

Sungura
~ and ~
Leopard

SUNGURA
and
LEOPARD
A SWAHILI TRICKSTER TALE

BARBARA KNUTSON

Little, Brown and Company
Boston   Toronto   London

First Edition

Library of Congress Cataloging-in-Publication Data
Knutson, Barbara.
  Sungura and Leopard : a Swahili trickster tale / Barbara Knutson. — 1st ed.
    p.   cm.
  Summary: A small but clever hare and a fierce leopard agree to share a house,
but as the hare's family grows, he realizes that he must find a way
to get rid of his bad-tempered neighbor.
  ISBN 0-316-50010-0
  [1. Folklore — Africa. 2. Hares — Folklore. 3. Leopards — Folklore.]
I. Title.
PZ8.1.K728Su 1993
398.24'529322 — dc20
[E]   92-31905

10 9 8 7 6 5 4 3 2 1
WOR

Published simultaneously in Canada
by Little, Brown & Company (Canada) Limited

Printed in the United States of America

The paintings in this book were done in ink and watercolor
on Canson scratchboard.

For Lindiwe

AUTHOR'S NOTE

The hare, called Sungura (soon-GOOR-a) in Swahili, is a common trickster in tales from East Africa. In folklore a trickster is a smaller animal who usually (but not always!) manages to outwit its neighbors, especially the bigger, fiercer ones. These stories have lasted for centuries because their message to ordinary people is that you don't have to be bigger or stronger than the people and forces "above" you — just smarter!

This retelling is based on a story from Tanzania, but I have also encountered another version of the same tale from the neighboring country of Malawi. I've always found it fascinating how a folktale can surface in different versions in various regions, and this book continues that tradition.

With a rich sense of family, Africans often honor relatives for many years after they have died and still feel connected with them. That is why, in this story, Sungura and Leopard are so happy to conclude that their ancestors agree with their choice of a site and even help with the building.

It used to be that Leopard lived alone in the bush. He would snarl at the rain when it spotted his spots and shove his way into other animals' homes to keep dry, but no one wanted to share a house with such a fierce, bad-tempered animal. In the end there was nothing for it but to make a house of his own. He searched and searched until he found the perfect place to build — a grassy clearing on a hill right by the river.

"Hmf! Not too bad!" Leopard grunted. "I'll be able to see any small animals for miles. There's nothing better than easy hunting." He licked his lips at the thought and set off to cut some long sticks for the frame of his new house.

Now, Sungura the hare also lived in the bush, and he just happened to decide the same thing as Leopard. "I need a real house. I've had enough of living in the bush without a roof over my ears," he said to himself.

He also went to search for a building site, and do you know what he found? A wonderful grassy clearing on a hill right by the river . . . and off he went to cut some branches to begin *his* house. "High on a hill!" He tapped his feet in a little dance as he went. "I'll be able to see any fierce animals for miles around. What a safe place to build a home!"

When Sungura came back with his bundle of sticks, he found another bundle already lying in the clearing. "Where did these come from?" he wondered. "I'm sure they weren't here before!"

He stroked his whiskers thoughtfully. "Why, of course! It must be my ancestors who are helping me. How kind of them! Those sticks are just the size I need to build my walls. Now all I need is some clay to plaster over the frame." Sungura hurried through the long grass down to the riverbank.

   While the hare was gone, Leopard came up the hill with his next load of wood. "Two!" he panted as he put down his pile. He stopped suddenly. Was there an extra bundle here? "One, two ... what comes after two? Four? Or is it seven? Drat this counting business!" hc snorted. "Well, I must be working more quickly than I thought, and that's good." But he was still frowning as he went to get some mud ready to plaster over the sticks.

When Leopard came back and found the frame already built, he knew there was more to this mystery than just counting wrong. He sat staring at the strong, straight poles woven together. Suddenly an idea came to him. "It must be that my ancestors are helping me!" he said, amazed. "What a good sign!" And he set to work harder than usual, relieved that he didn't have to count anymore.

So it went,

Sungura and Leopard

never seeing each other

while building the same house.

In fact, they worked so hard and so quickly that they finished in the dark that very night.

It was a fine home, with sturdy walls and a thatched roof so thick that even under the shimmering African stars, it was as black as a cave inside.

The hare and the leopard could hardly see their own paws in front of them as they each crawled in, tired as could be, and went straight to sleep without a sound.

The next morning, what do you suppose they discovered when the sun came up? I tell you, there were two surprised animals in that hut!

Leopard growled fiercely. "Get out of my house, Sungura!" He always talked before thinking.

Sungura was too angry to be frightened. "Ho! *Your* house, Leopard? I built this house, and what's more, my ancestors helped me. I think it's you who should leave."

"Don't try to trick me, Sungura," Leopard snarled. "It was *I* who built this house with the help of *my* ancestors."

"*Your* ancestors? Wait a minute, wait a minute!" Sungura held up a paw. "I think I see what happened here. We *both* built this house, without any ancestors at all! Well, I refuse to leave after all the work I've done! And if you won't leave" — the leopard only growled at that — "then we will have to divide it between us."

Leopard fussed and fumed, but he finally had to admit that Sungura was right. So that is how Leopard and Sungura ended up each living on one side of the hut with just a thin wall between them.

It was not long before Sungura had a big happy family living on his side. Leopard was annoyed. Less peace and quiet than ever!

As for Sungura, he was nervous, living next to someone so much bigger and fiercer than himself. When would Leopard

suddenly lose his temper and snatch up Sungura or his wife or one of their children? He seemed to be looking rather grouchy these days. The hare and his wife began to think of a way to get their dangerous neighbor safely out of the way.

One morning as Leopard woke up, he could hear Sungura's children in the next room, crying and whimpering. "Drat those hares!" he grumbled. "Why don't they keep quiet so I can sleep? One of these days I'm going to put a stop to this and have dinner in the bargain." He turned over and tried to doze off again, but now he could hear Sungura talking loudly to his wife.

"What is the matter with our children this morning?" the hare was asking. "Why are they crying like this?"

She replied just as loudly. "They're *so* hungry, Sungura. We've finished all of the elephant meat you brought home last week."

"Elephant meat!" Leopard gasped as he pressed his ear to the wall. "Ai, those greedy children!" Sungura was saying, "I suppose I must go and hunt more elephant today. What a nuisance!"

Leopard's whiskers were trembling. Perhaps his neighbor was fiercer than he had realized. Leopard stepped very softly around the house that day so that he wouldn't annoy any of the hares.

But nothing more happened. In fact, by the end of the week, Leopard was starting to remember that Sungura was, after all, a rather small animal, and that he, Leopard, wouldn't mind having the whole house to himself. He began to look rather hungrily at the baby hares as they played outside the door.

The next morning, Leopard again woke up to hear the hare's children whimpering, then sobbing, then wailing even worse than before. Sungura and his wife were talking more loudly and clearly than ever.

"Sungura!" His wife was fairly shouting. "The children are so hungry for leopard meat. They really must have some or they will never stop crying."

"Ai! Those children of ours!" cried Sungura. "I suppose I'll have to get them some leopard meat today, or we'll never have peace."

On the other side of the wall, Leopard was shaking so much he was afraid his spots would fall off. La! What a neighbor! If Sungura could kill elephants, he could certainly make short work of a leopard.

There was no time to lose. Slinking out of the house, Leopard scrambled quickly into the bushes at the edge of the clearing. "Safe!" he breathed to himself.

"Safe!" said the hares to each other as they watched from their half of the doorway. "At last Leopard is gone!"

Sungura picked up a hoe and chopped the first little chink out of the wall that divided the house. The children cheered. But suddenly the smallest hare shrieked and pointed down the hill in alarm. What was this? Here came Leopard out of the bush again, back toward the house. And who was with him? That rascally Baboon! They could even hear him telling Leopard as the two came up the hill, "Really, Leopard, that Sungura would trick anybody. How could you believe that a small animal like him would try to attack you?" Leopard still didn't look too sure, but he was coming closer and closer.

"Quick! A plan!" Sungura's wife whispered as Baboon left
and Leopard padded cautiously back into his side of the house.

"Hmf!" Leopard coughed uneasily. "I suppose Baboon is right about Sungura. A very small animal, after all." He coughed again to reassure himself and unrolled his favorite mat.

Sungura waited until he heard Leopard settling down next to the wall. "Well, my dear," he said loudly, "Leopard should be back soon. How clever of you to send Baboon to trick him into coming back! Don't cry, children. Soon you'll have your leopard meat after all."

But the children weren't crying at all. In fact they were laughing and peering out of the door to see the end of Leopard's tail disappearing into the bush. And do you know what?

He hasn't been back since.